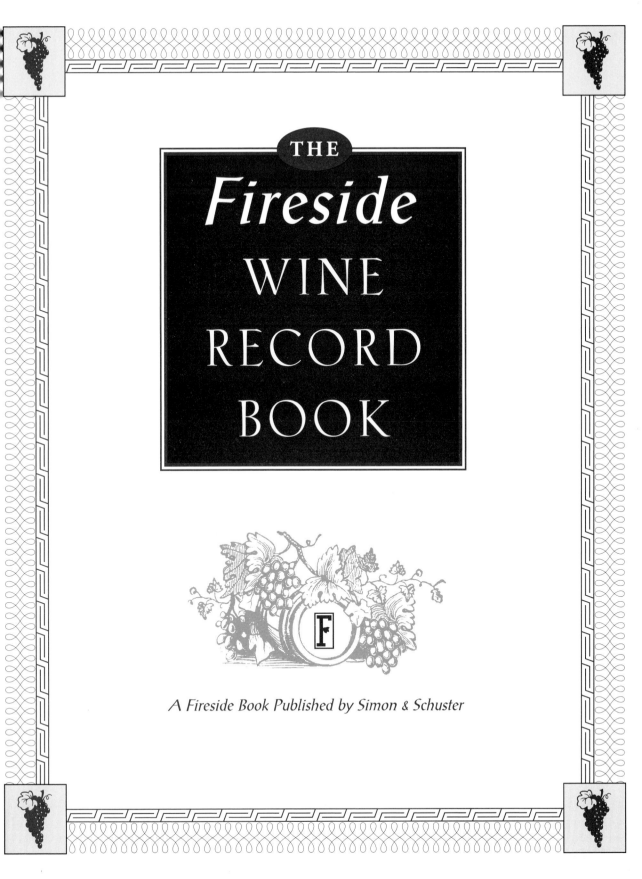

THE

Fireside
WINE
RECORD
BOOK

A Fireside Book Published by Simon & Schuster

Name of Wine

Bottled By

Vintage

Region

Bought at

Price   Quantity

Date

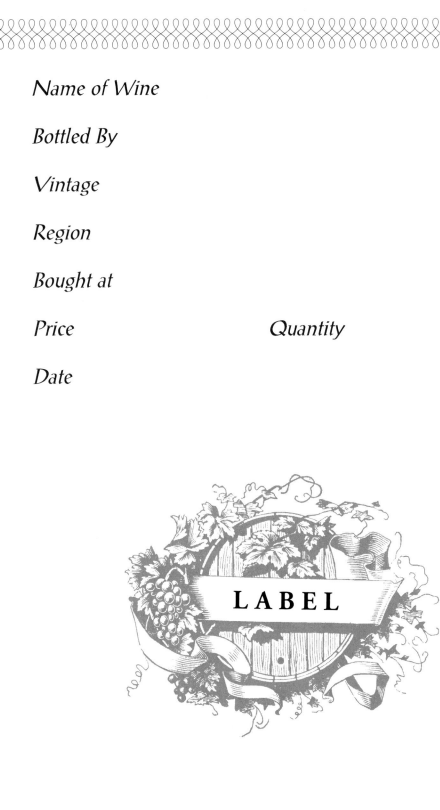

LABEL

Opened on

Place

Menu

Color

Bouquet

Taste

Remarks

Name of Wine

Bottled By

Vintage

Region

Bought at

Price   Quantity

Date

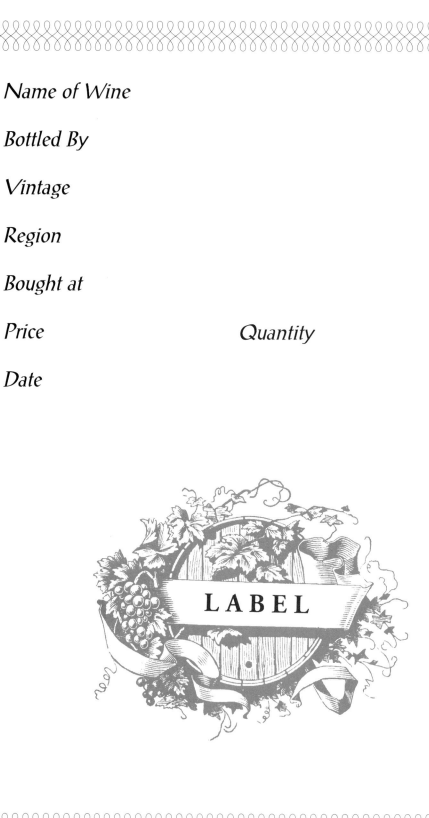

Opened on

Place

Menu

Color

Bouquet

Taste

Remarks

Name of Wine

Bottled By

Vintage

Region

Bought at

Price   Quantity

Date

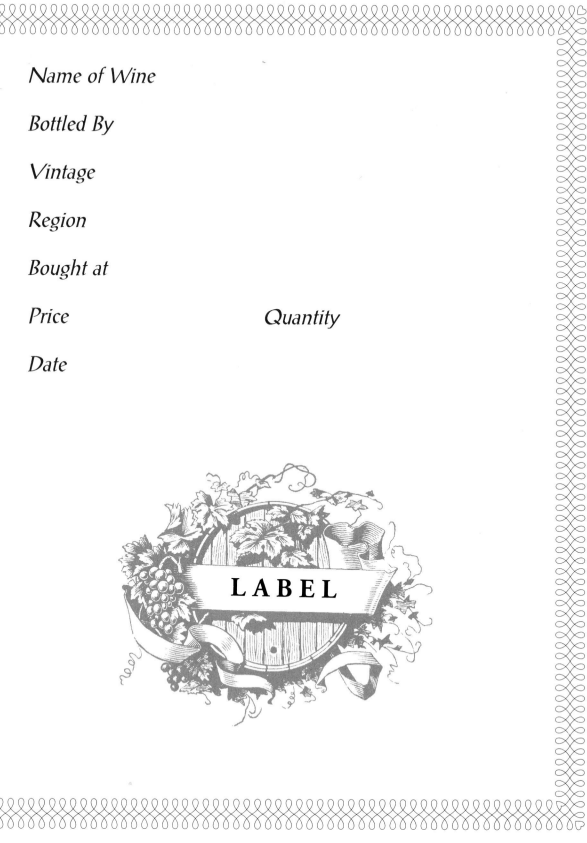

LABEL

Opened on

Place

Menu

Color

Bouquet

Taste

Remarks

Name of Wine

Bottled By

Vintage

Region

Bought at

Price   Quantity

Date

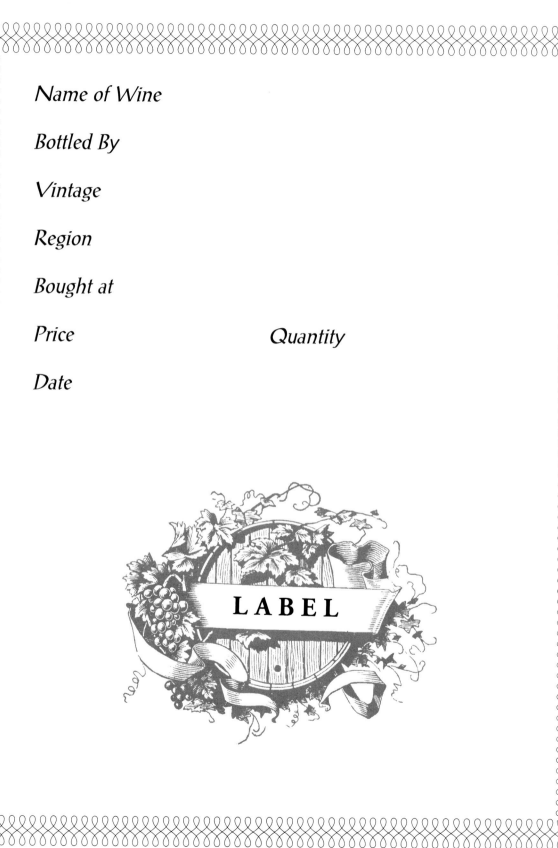

Opened on

Place

Menu

Color

Bouquet

Taste

Remarks

Name of Wine

Bottled By

Vintage

Region

Bought at

Price   Quantity

Date

LABEL

Opened on

Place

Menu

Color

Bouquet

Taste

Remarks

Name of Wine

Bottled By

Vintage

Region

Bought at

Price   *Quantity*

Date

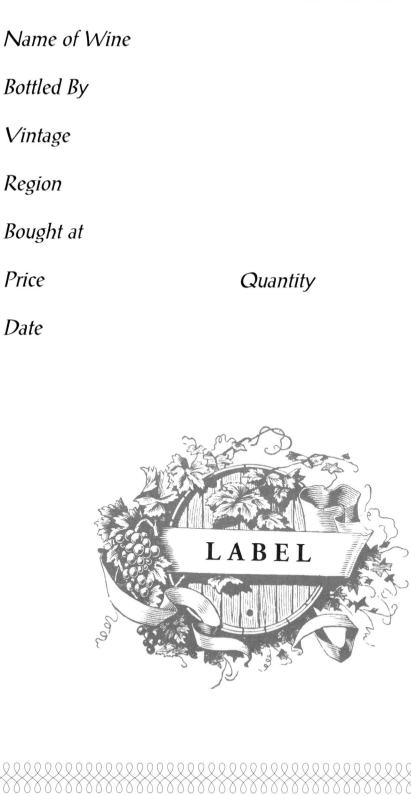

LABEL

Opened on

Place

Menu

Color

Bouquet

Taste

Remarks

Name of Wine

Bottled By

Vintage

Region

Bought at

Price   Quantity

Date

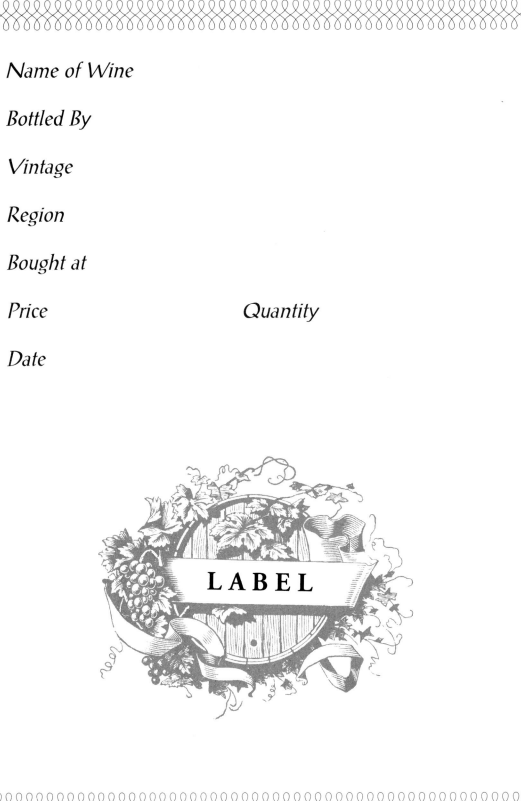

Opened on

Place

Menu

Color

Bouquet

Taste

Remarks

Name of Wine

Bottled By

Vintage

Region

Bought at

Price *Quantity*

Date

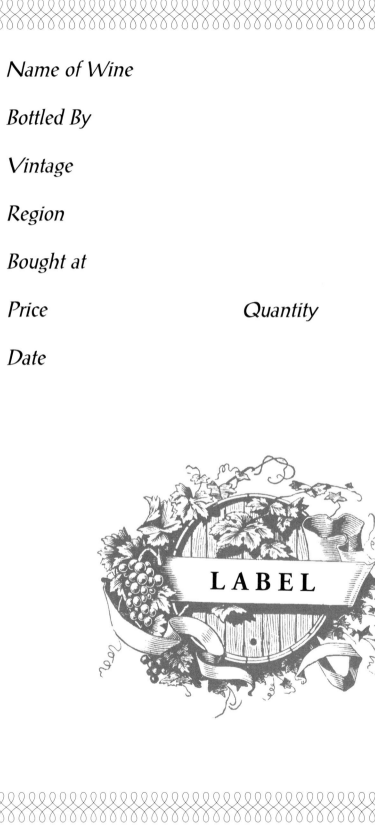

LABEL

Opened on

Place

Menu

Color

Bouquet

Taste

Remarks

Name of Wine

Bottled By

Vintage

Region

Bought at

Price   Quantity

Date

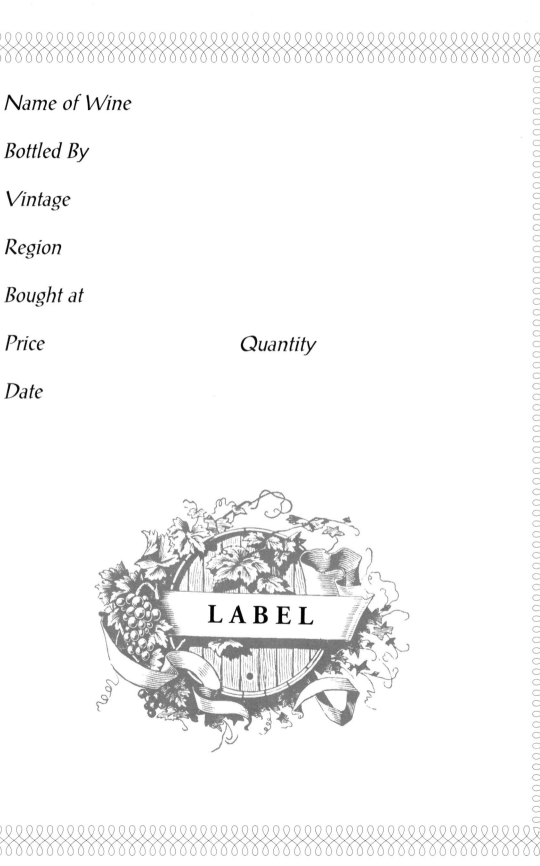

Opened on

Place

Menu

Color

Bouquet

Taste

Remarks

Name of Wine

Bottled By

Vintage

Region

Bought at

Price   Quantity

Date

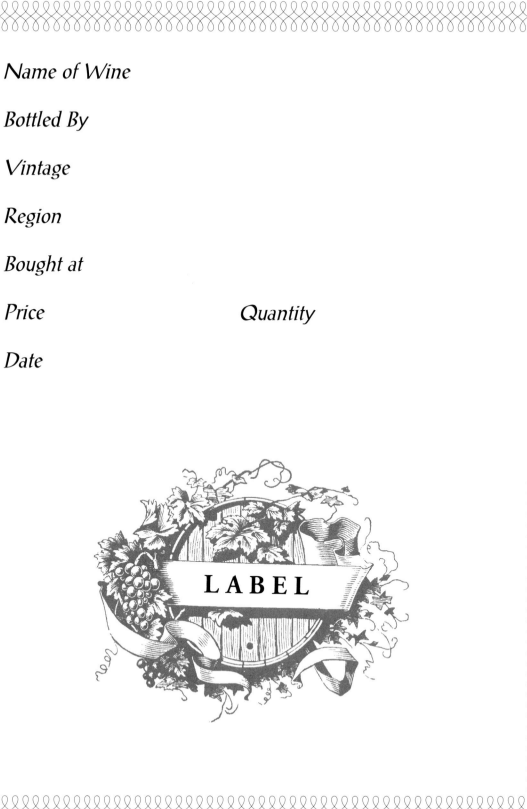

LABEL

Opened on

Place

Menu

Color

Bouquet

Taste

Remarks

Name of Wine

Bottled By

Vintage

Region

Bought at

Price   Quantity

Date

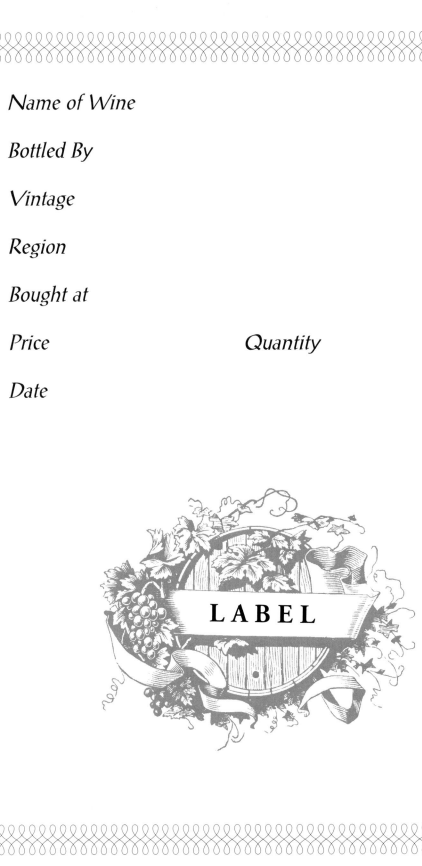

LABEL

Opened on

Place

Menu

Color

Bouquet

Taste

Remarks

Name of Wine

Bottled By

Vintage

Region

Bought at

Price   Quantity

Date

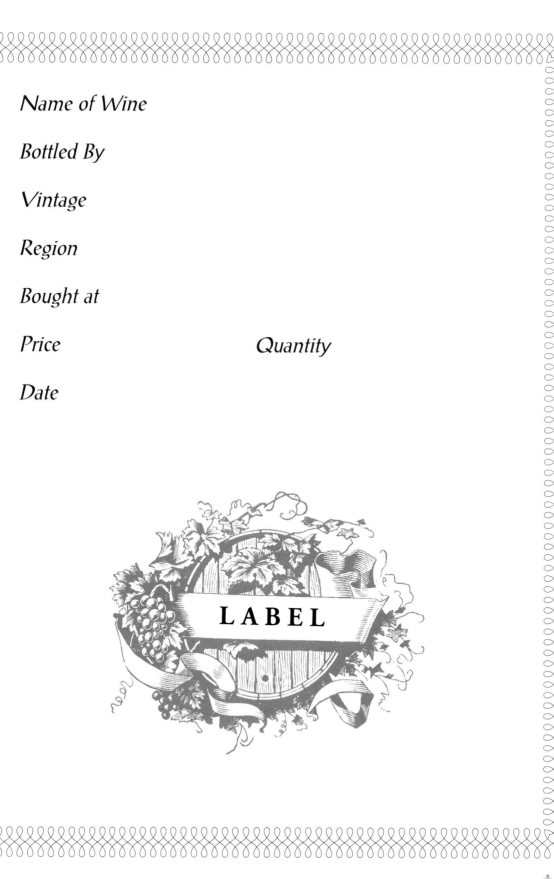

LABEL

Opened on

Place

Menu

Color

Bouquet

Taste

Remarks

Name of Wine

Bottled By

Vintage

Region

Bought at

Price   Quantity

Date

LABEL

Opened on

Place

Menu

Color

Bouquet

Taste

Remarks

Name of Wine

Bottled By

Vintage

Region

Bought at

Price   Quantity

Date

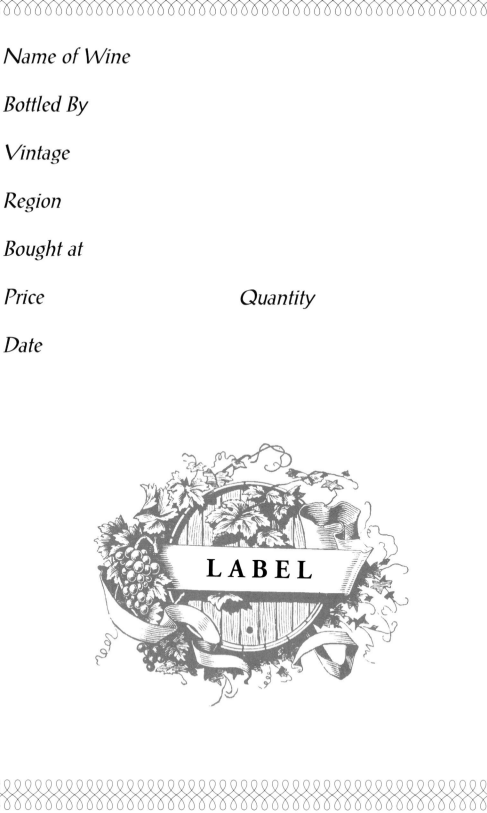

LABEL

Opened on

Place

Menu

Color

Bouquet

Taste

Remarks

Name of Wine

Bottled By

Vintage

Region

Bought at

Price   Quantity

Date

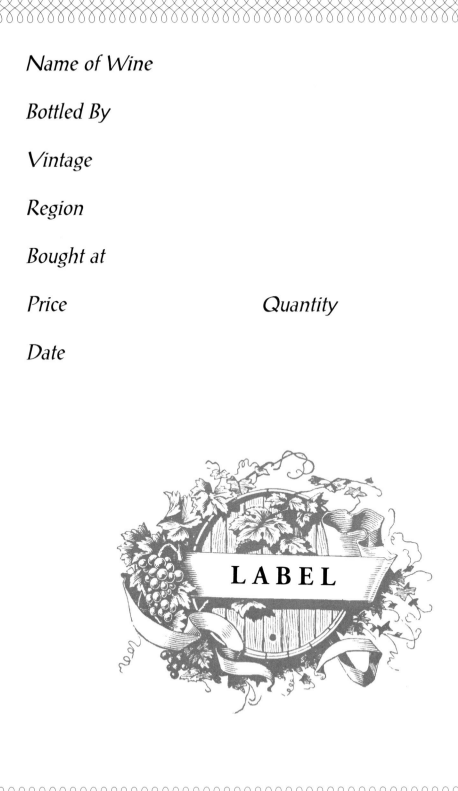

LABEL

Opened on

Place

Menu

Color

Bouquet

Taste

Remarks

Name of Wine

Bottled By

Vintage

Region

Bought at

Price   Quantity

Date

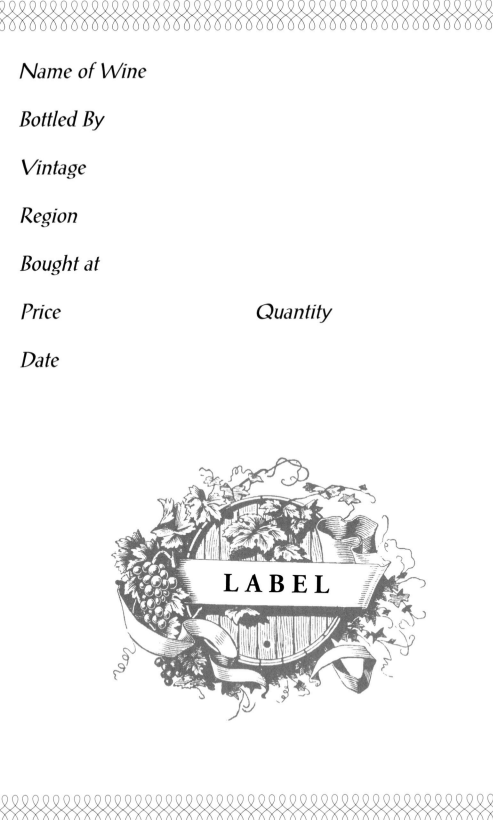

LABEL

Opened on

Place

Menu

Color

Bouquet

Taste

Remarks

Name of Wine

Bottled By

Vintage

Region

Bought at

Price   Quantity

Date

Opened on

Place

Menu

Color

Bouquet

Taste

Remarks

Name of Wine

Bottled By

Vintage

Region

Bought at

Price   *Quantity*

Date

LABEL

Opened on

Place

Menu

Color

Bouquet

Taste

Remarks

Name of Wine

Bottled By

Vintage

Region

Bought at

Price   *Quantity*

Date

LABEL

Opened on

Place

Menu

Color

Bouquet

Taste

Remarks

Name of Wine

Bottled By

Vintage

Region

Bought at

Price   Quantity

Date

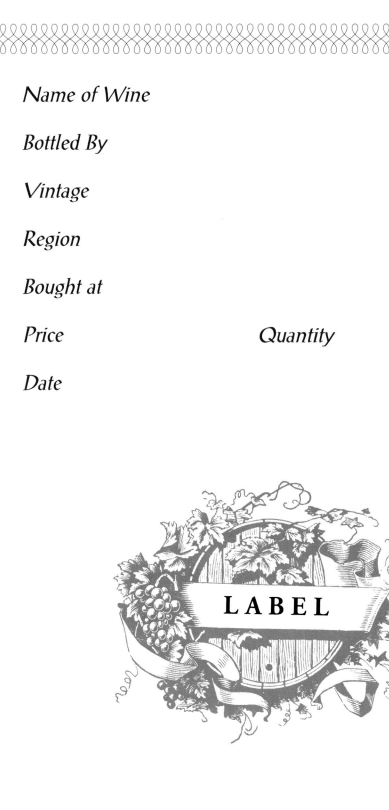

Opened on

Place

Menu

Color

Bouquet

Taste

Remarks

Name of Wine

Bottled By

Vintage

Region

Bought at

Price   Quantity

Date

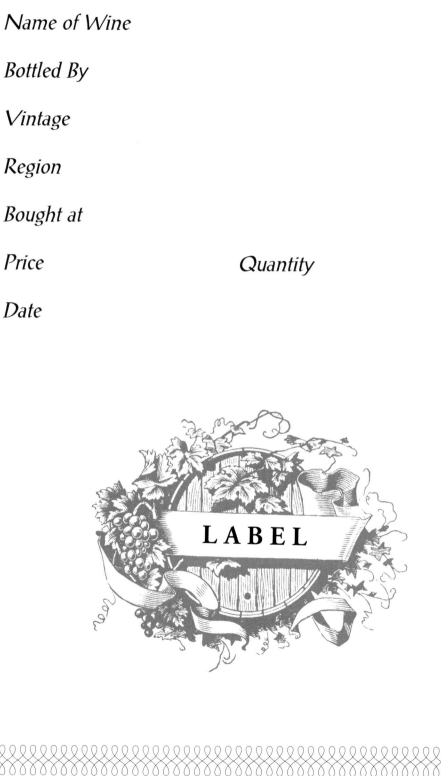

LABEL

Opened on

Place

Menu

Color

Bouquet

Taste

Remarks

Name of Wine

Bottled By

Vintage

Region

Bought at

Price   Quantity

Date

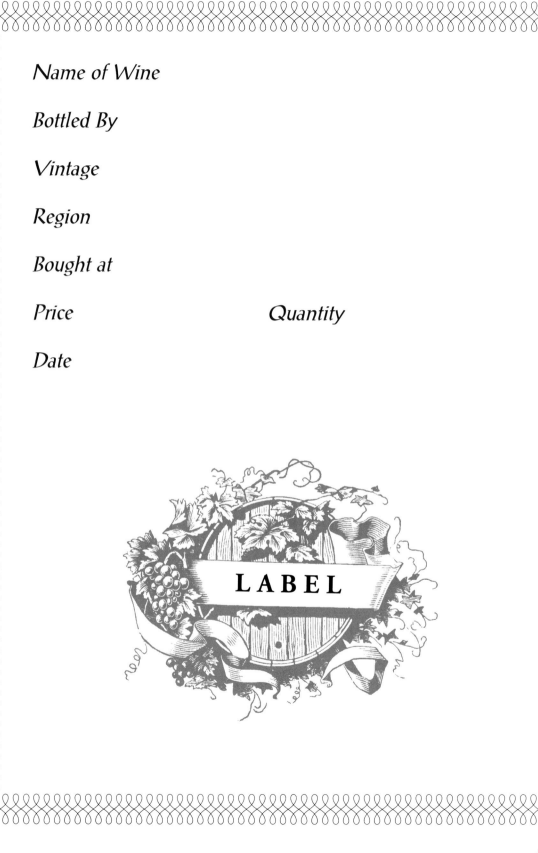

LABEL

Opened on

Place

Menu

Color

Bouquet

Taste

Remarks

Name of Wine

Bottled By

Vintage

Region

Bought at

Price   *Quantity*

Date

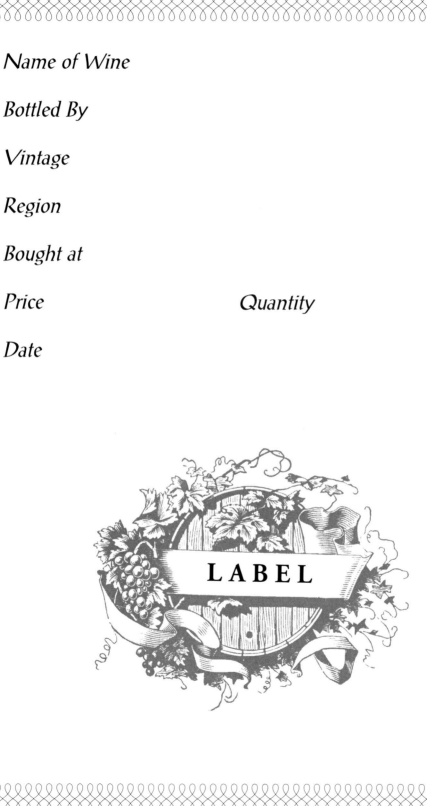

LABEL

Opened on

Place

Menu

Color

Bouquet

Taste

Remarks

Name of Wine

Bottled By

Vintage

Region

Bought at

Price   Quantity

Date

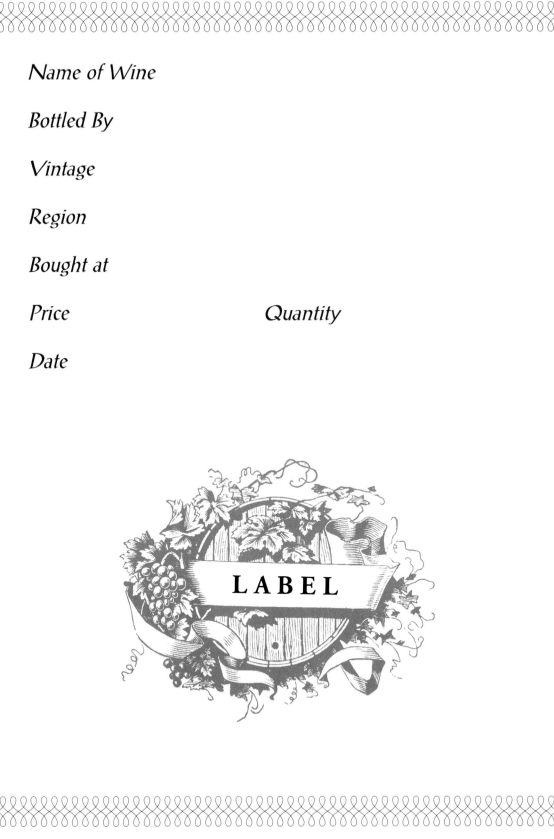

Opened on

Place

Menu

Color

Bouquet

Taste

Remarks

Name of Wine

Bottled By

Vintage

Region

Bought at

Price   Quantity

Date

LABEL

Opened on

Place

Menu

Color

Bouquet

Taste

Remarks

Name of Wine

Bottled By

Vintage

Region

Bought at

Price   Quantity

Date

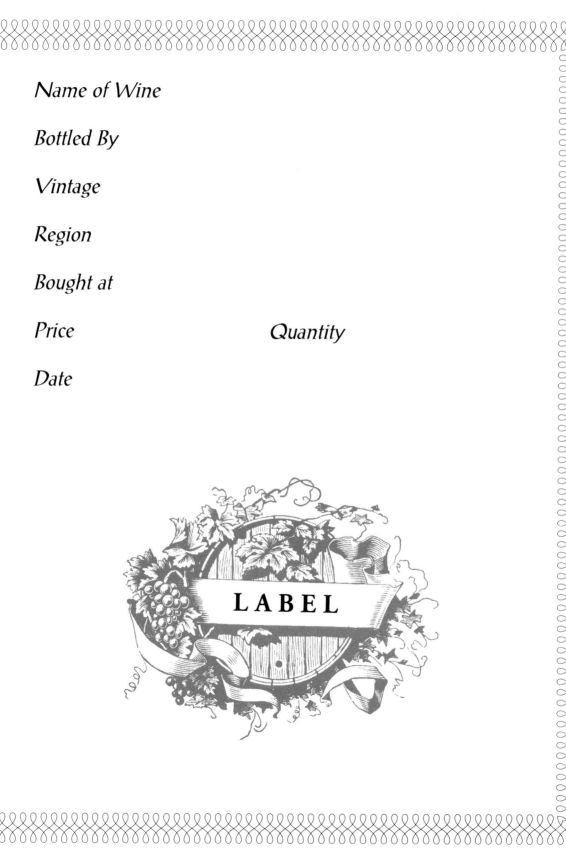

LABEL

Opened on

Place

Menu

Color

Bouquet

Taste

Remarks

Name of Wine

Bottled By

Vintage

Region

Bought at

Price   Quantity

Date

LABEL

Opened on

Place

Menu

Color

Bouquet

Taste

Remarks

Name of Wine

Bottled By

Vintage

Region

Bought at

Price   Quantity

Date

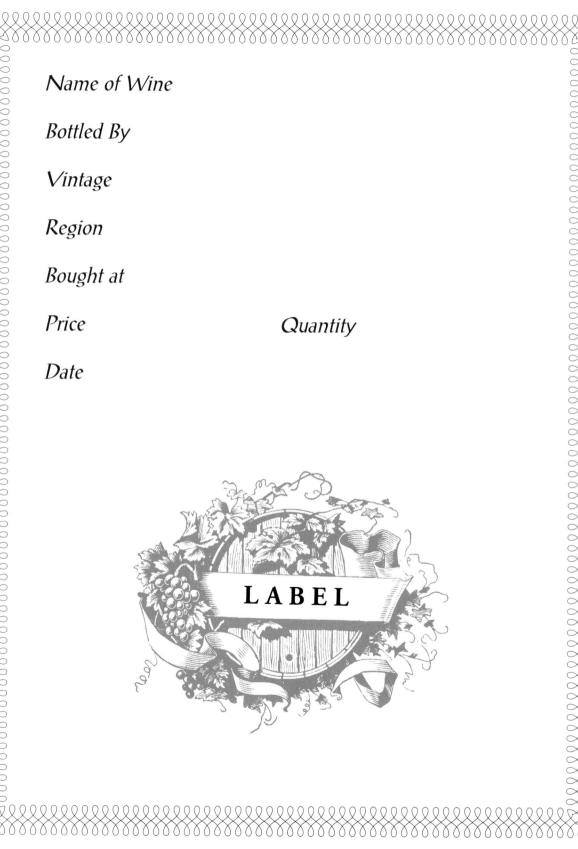

LABEL

Opened on

Place

Menu

Color

Bouquet

Taste

Remarks

Name of Wine

Bottled By

Vintage

Region

Bought at

Price   Quantity

Date

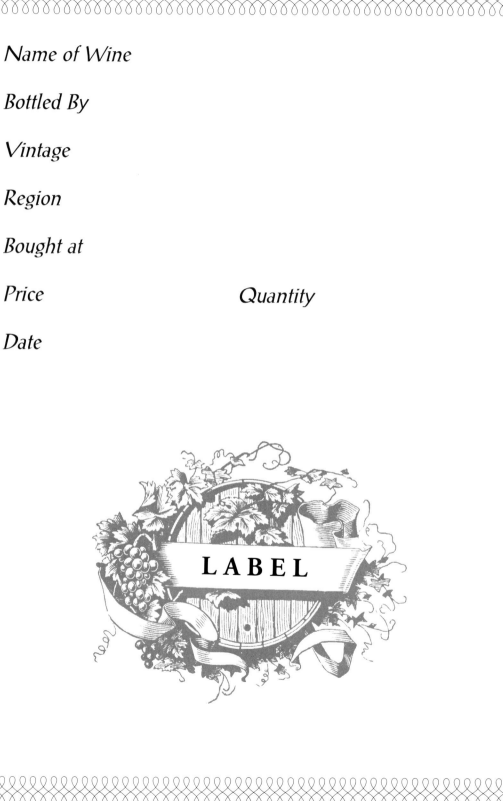

LABEL

Opened on

Place

Menu

Color

Bouquet

Taste

Remarks

Name of Wine

Bottled By

Vintage

Region

Bought at

Price   Quantity

Date

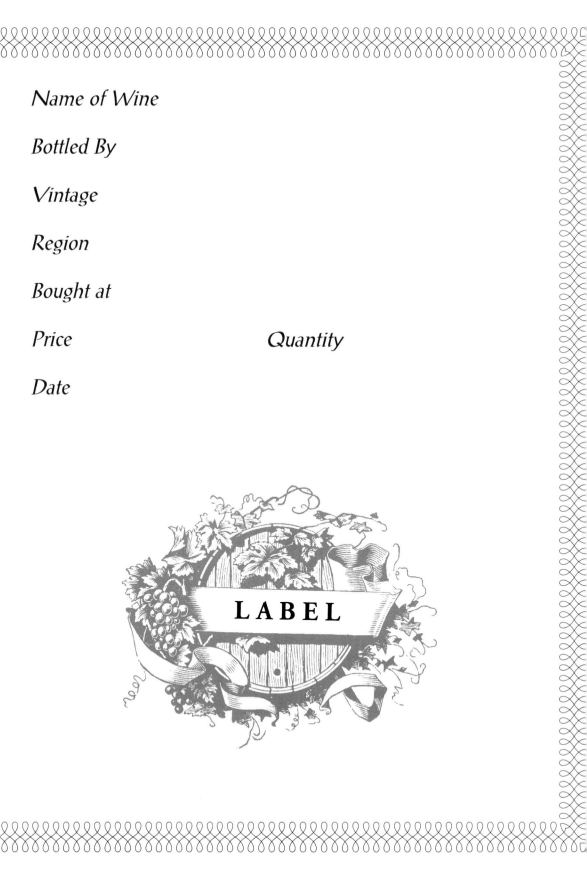

LABEL

Opened on

Place

Menu

Color

Bouquet

Taste

Remarks

Name of Wine

Bottled By

Vintage

Region

Bought at

Price   Quantity

Date

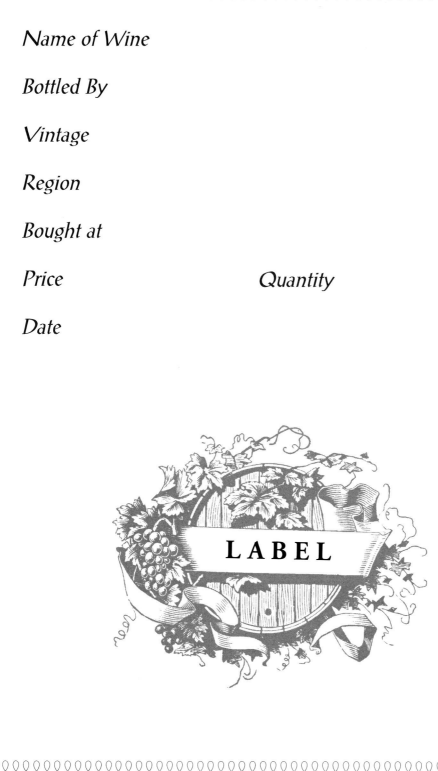

LABEL

Opened on

Place

Menu

Color

Bouquet

Taste

Remarks

Name of Wine

Bottled By

Vintage

Region

Bought at

Price   Quantity

Date

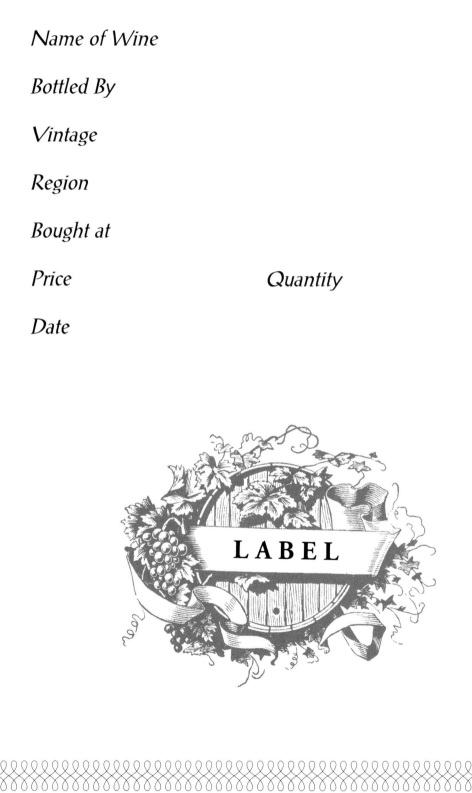

LABEL

Opened on

Place

Menu

Color

Bouquet

Taste

Remarks

Name of Wine

Bottled By

Vintage

Region

Bought at

Price   Quantity

Date

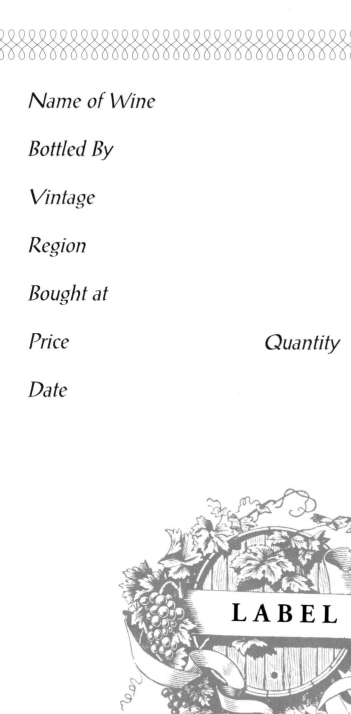

LABEL

Opened on

Place

Menu

Color

Bouquet

Taste

Remarks

Name of Wine

Bottled By

Vintage

Region

Bought at

Price   Quantity

Date

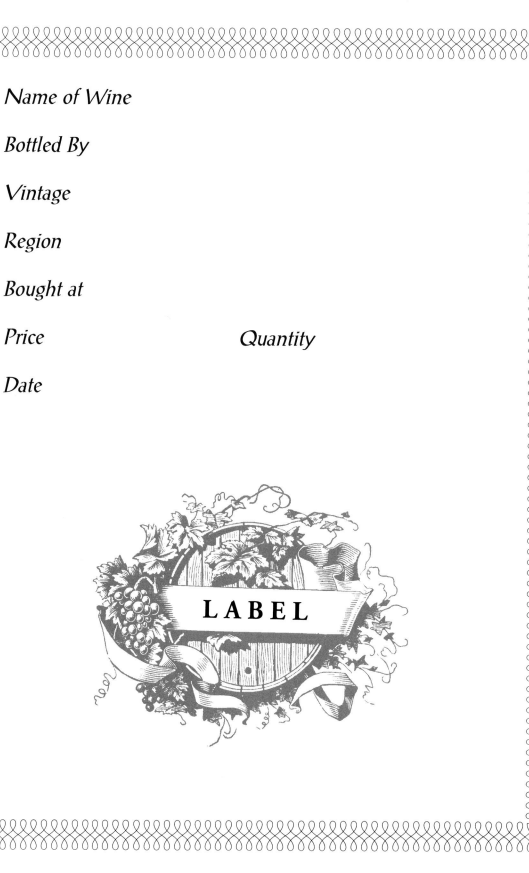

LABEL

Opened on

Place

Menu

Color

Bouquet

Taste

Remarks

Name of Wine

Bottled By

Vintage

Region

Bought at

Price   Quantity

Date

LABEL

Opened on

Place

Menu

Color

Bouquet

Taste

Remarks

Name of Wine

Bottled By

Vintage

Region

Bought at

Price   Quantity

Date

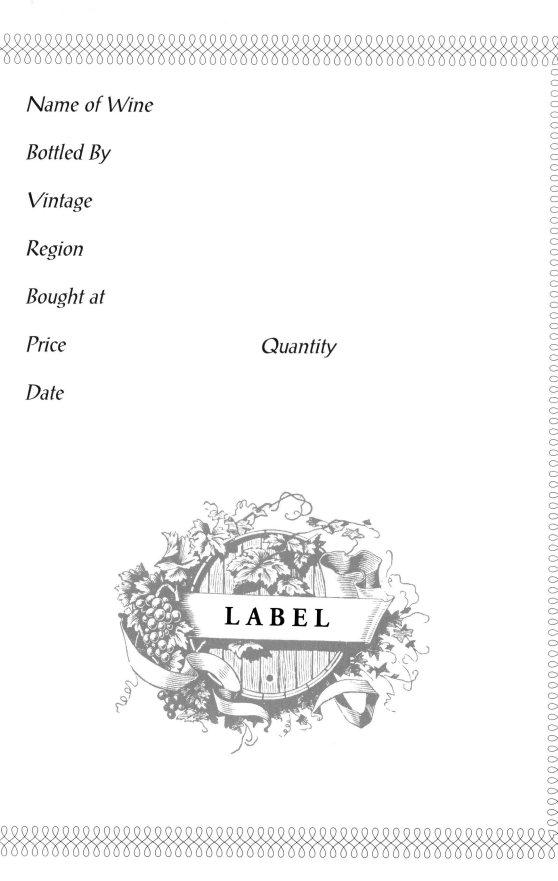

LABEL

Opened on

Place

Menu

Color

Bouquet

Taste

Remarks

Name of Wine

Bottled By

Vintage

Region

Bought at

Price   Quantity

Date

Opened on

Place

Menu

Color

Bouquet

Taste

Remarks

Name of Wine

Bottled By

Vintage

Region

Bought at

Price   Quantity

Date

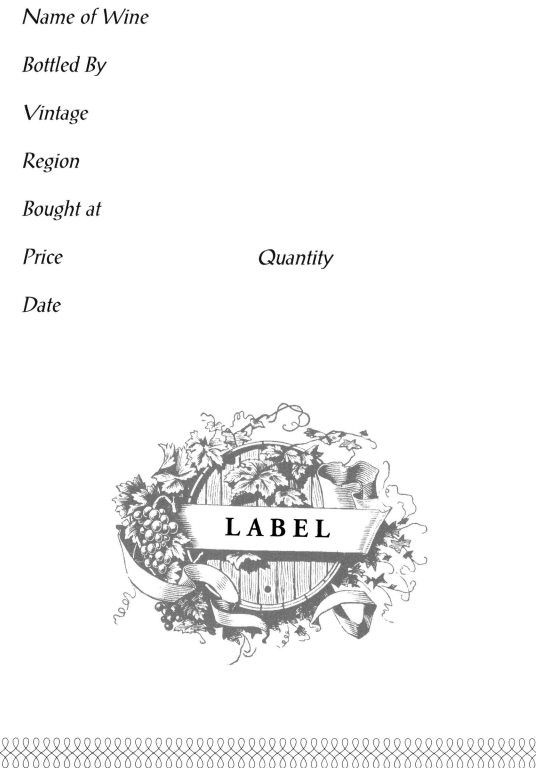

Opened on

Place

Menu

Color

Bouquet

Taste

Remarks

Name of Wine

Bottled By

Vintage

Region

Bought at

Price   *Quantity*

Date

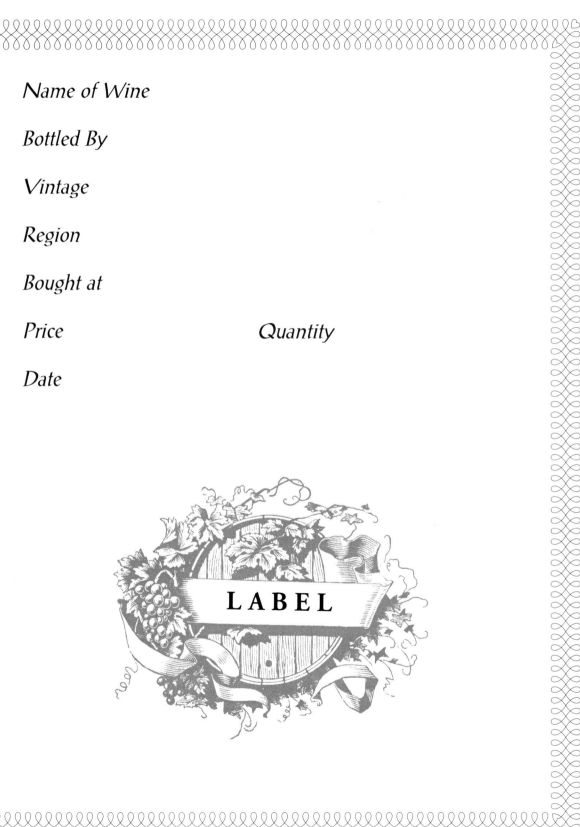

LABEL

Opened on

Place

Menu

Color

Bouquet

Taste

Remarks

Name of Wine

Bottled By

Vintage

Region

Bought at

Price   Quantity

Date

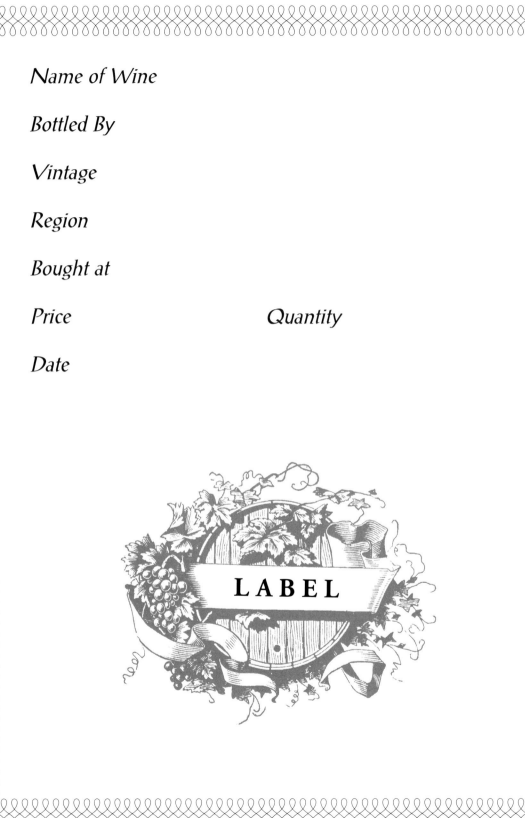

LABEL

Opened on

Place

Menu

Color

Bouquet

Taste

Remarks

Name of Wine

Bottled By

Vintage

Region

Bought at

Price   Quantity

Date

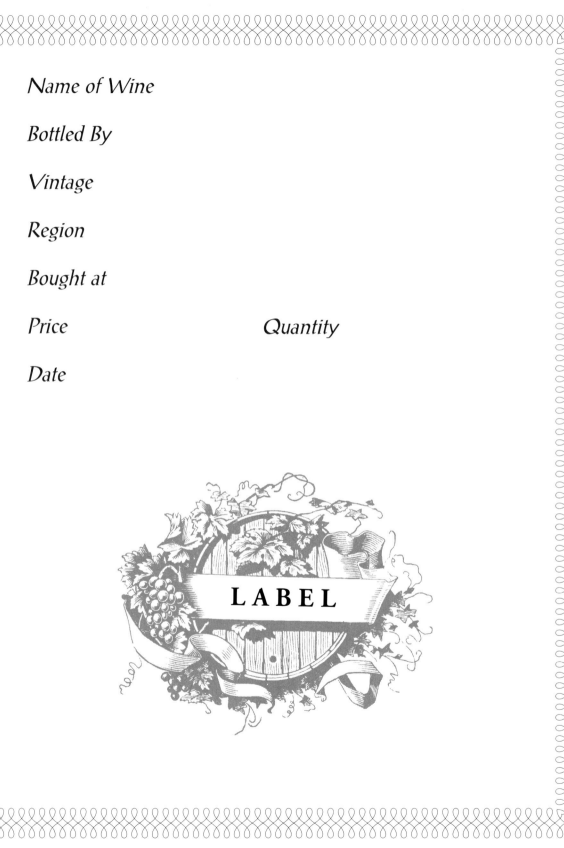

Opened on

Place

Menu

Color

Bouquet

Taste

Remarks

Name of Wine

Bottled By

Vintage

Region

Bought at

Price   Quantity

Date

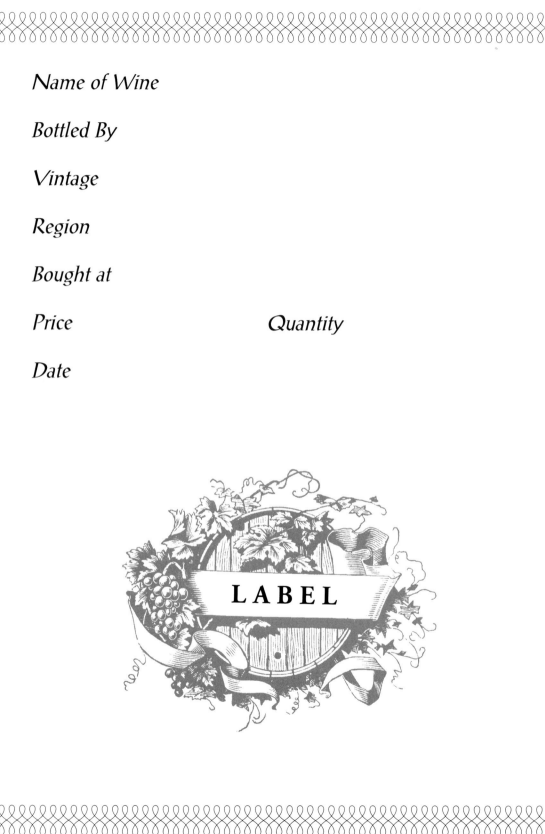

LABEL

Opened on

Place

Menu

Color

Bouquet

Taste

Remarks

Name of Wine

Bottled By

Vintage

Region

Bought at

Price   Quantity

Date

Opened on

Place

Menu

Color

Bouquet

Taste

Remarks

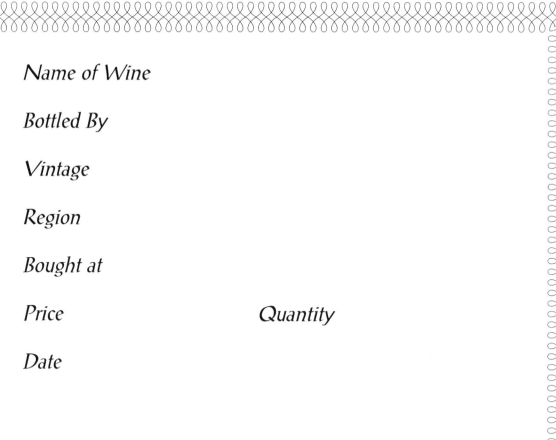

Name of Wine

Bottled By

Vintage

Region

Bought at

Price   Quantity

Date

LABEL

Opened on

Place

Menu

Color

Bouquet

Taste

Remarks

Name of Wine

Bottled By

Vintage

Region

Bought at

Price   Quantity

Date

LABEL

Opened on

Place

Menu

Color

Bouquet

Taste

Remarks

Name of Wine

Bottled By

Vintage

Region

Bought at

Price   Quantity

Date

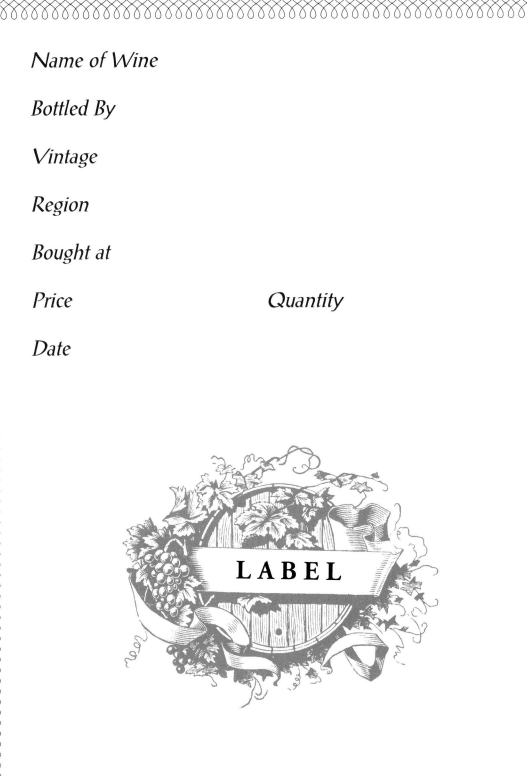

LABEL

Opened on

Place

Menu

Color

Bouquet

Taste

Remarks

Name of Wine

Bottled By

Vintage

Region

Bought at

Price   *Quantity*

Date

LABEL

Opened on

Place

Menu

Color

Bouquet

Taste

Remarks

Name of Wine

Bottled By

Vintage

Region

Bought at

Price   *Quantity*

Date

LABEL

Opened on

Place

Menu

Color

Bouquet

Taste

Remarks

Name of Wine

Bottled By

Vintage

Region

Bought at

Price   Quantity

Date

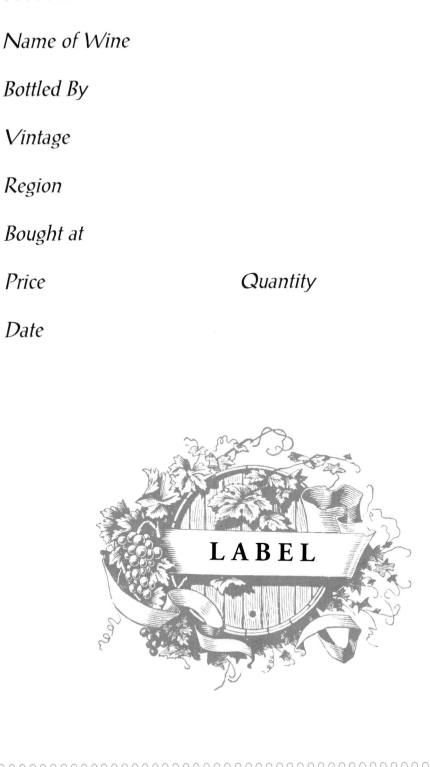

LABEL

Opened on

Place

Menu

Color

Bouquet

Taste

Remarks

Name of Wine

Bottled By

Vintage

Region

Bought at

Price   Quantity

Date

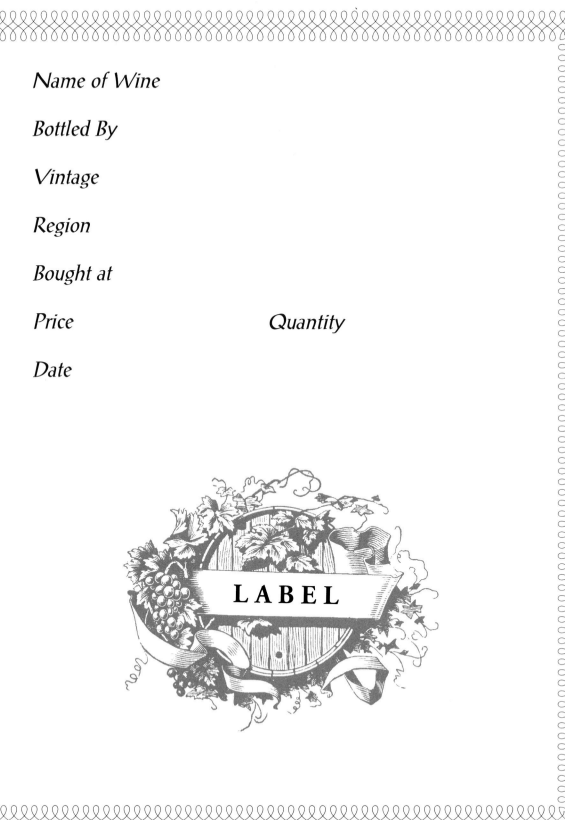

Opened on

Place

Menu

Color

Bouquet

Taste

Remarks

Name of Wine

Bottled By

Vintage

Region

Bought at

Price   Quantity

Date

LABEL

Opened on

Place

Menu

Color

Bouquet

Taste

Remarks

Name of Wine

Bottled By

Vintage

Region

Bought at

Price   Quantity

Date

LABEL

Opened on

Place

Menu

Color

Bouquet

Taste

Remarks

Name of Wine

Bottled By

Vintage

Region

Bought at

Price   Quantity

Date

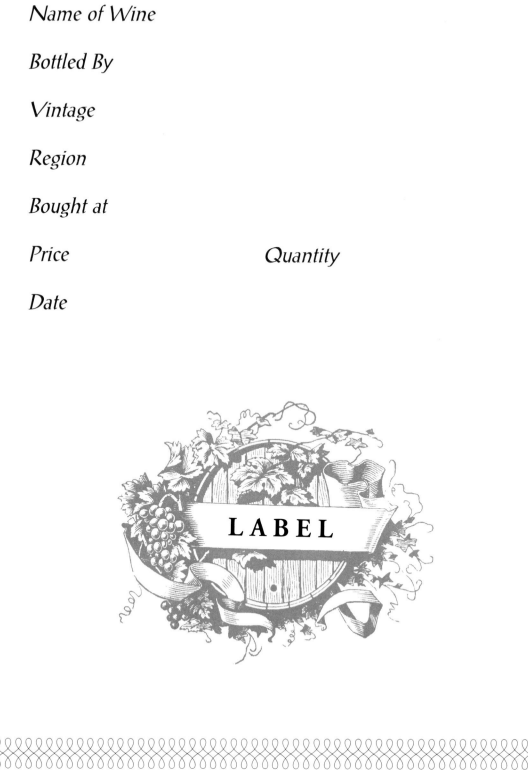

LABEL

Opened on

Place

Menu

Color

Bouquet

Taste

Remarks

Name of Wine

Bottled By

Vintage

Region

Bought at

Price   Quantity

Date

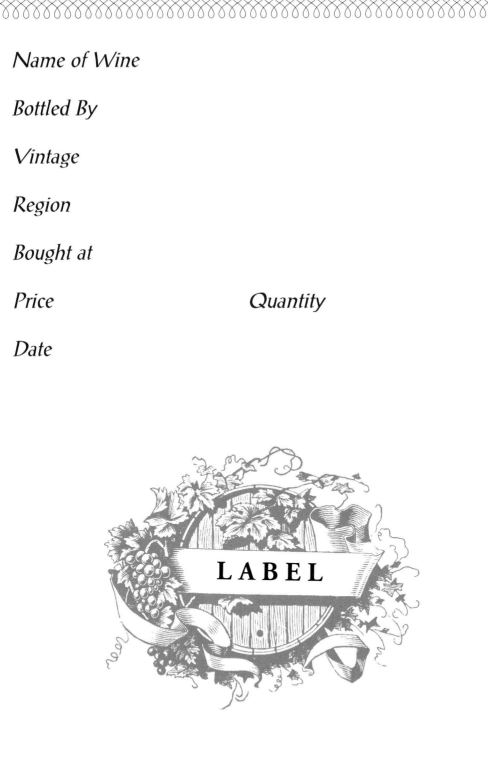

LABEL

Opened on

Place

Menu

Color

Bouquet

Taste

Remarks

Name of Wine

Bottled By

Vintage

Region

Bought at

Price   Quantity

Date

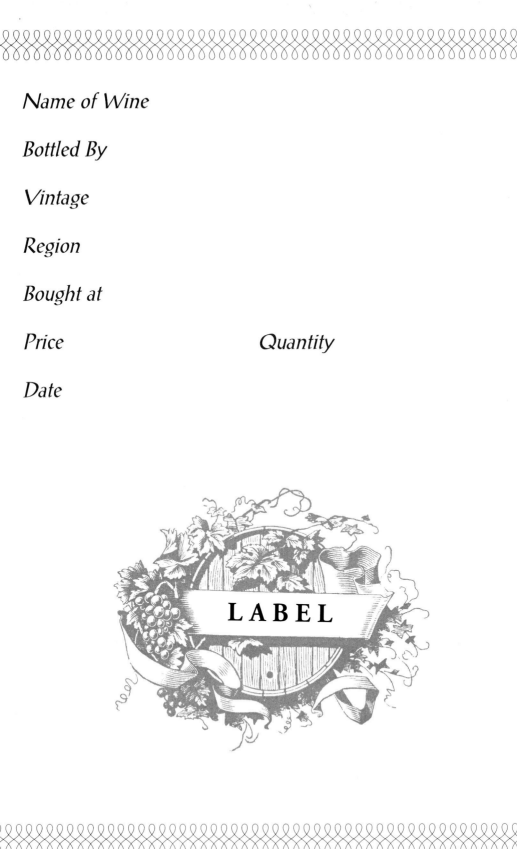

LABEL

Opened on

Place

Menu

Color

Bouquet

Taste

Remarks

Name of Wine

Bottled By

Vintage

Region

Bought at

Price   *Quantity*

Date

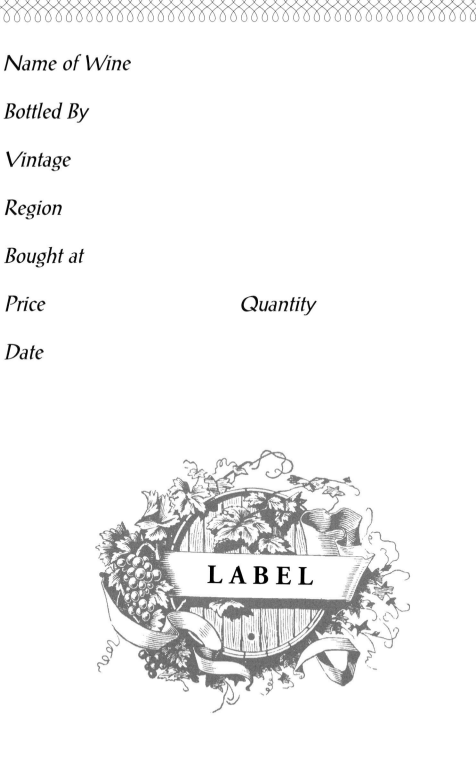

LABEL

Opened on

Place

Menu

Color

Bouquet

Taste

Remarks

Name of Wine

Bottled By

Vintage

Region

Bought at

Price   Quantity

Date

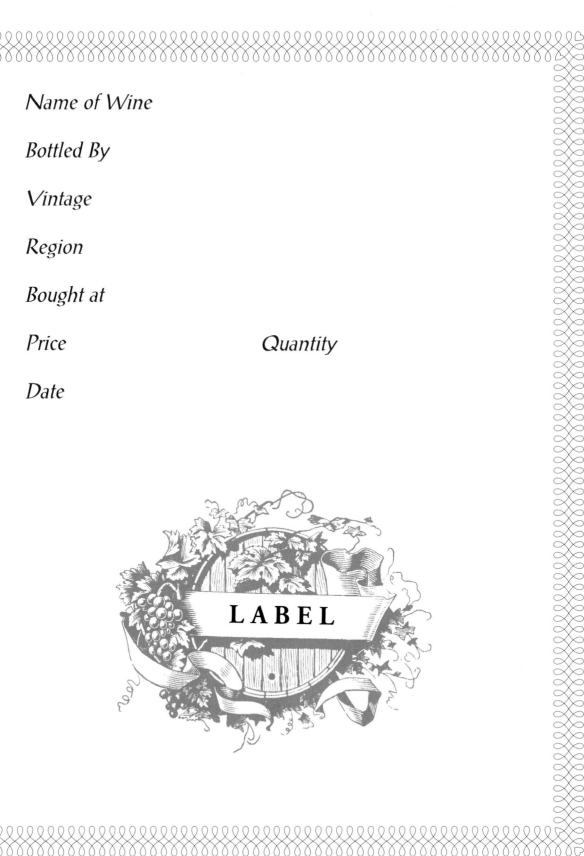

LABEL

Opened on

Place

Menu

Color

Bouquet

Taste

Remarks

Name of Wine

Bottled By

Vintage

Region

Bought at

Price   Quantity

Date

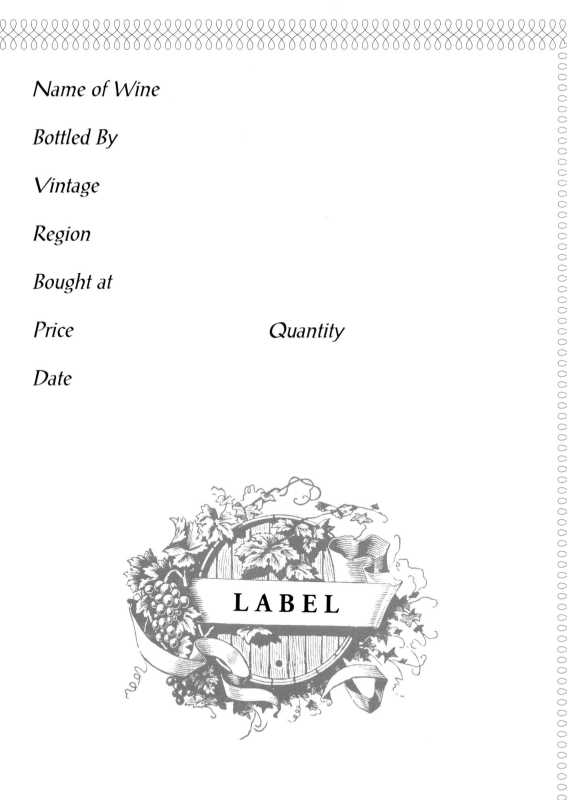

Opened on

Place

Menu

Color

Bouquet

Taste

Remarks

Name of Wine

Bottled By

Vintage

Region

Bought at

Price   Quantity

Date

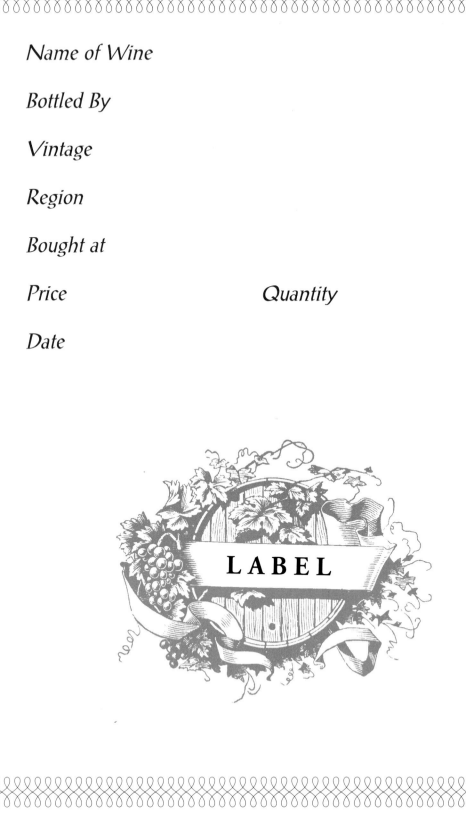

Opened on

Place

Menu

Color

Bouquet

Taste

Remarks

Name of Wine

Bottled By

Vintage

Region

Bought at

Price   Quantity

Date

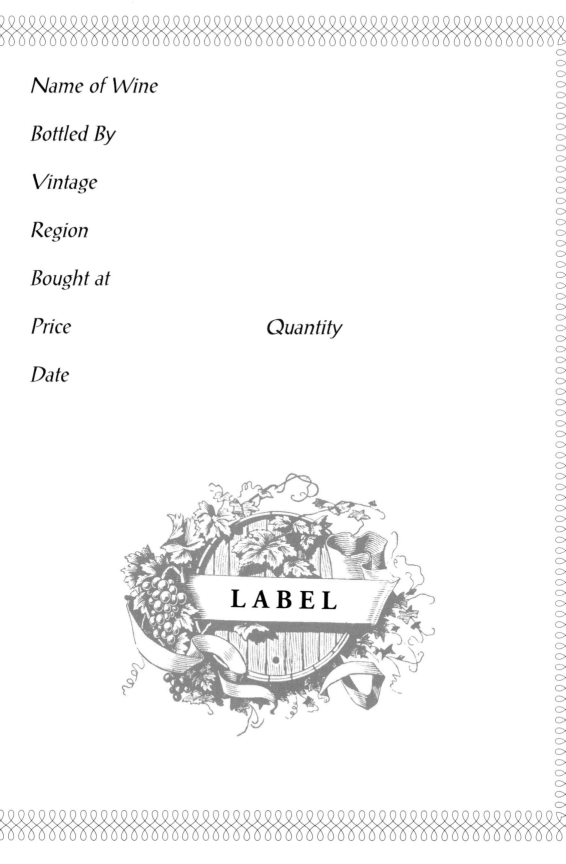

LABEL

Opened on

Place

Menu

Color

Bouquet

Taste

Remarks

Name of Wine

Bottled By

Vintage

Region

Bought at

Price   Quantity

Date

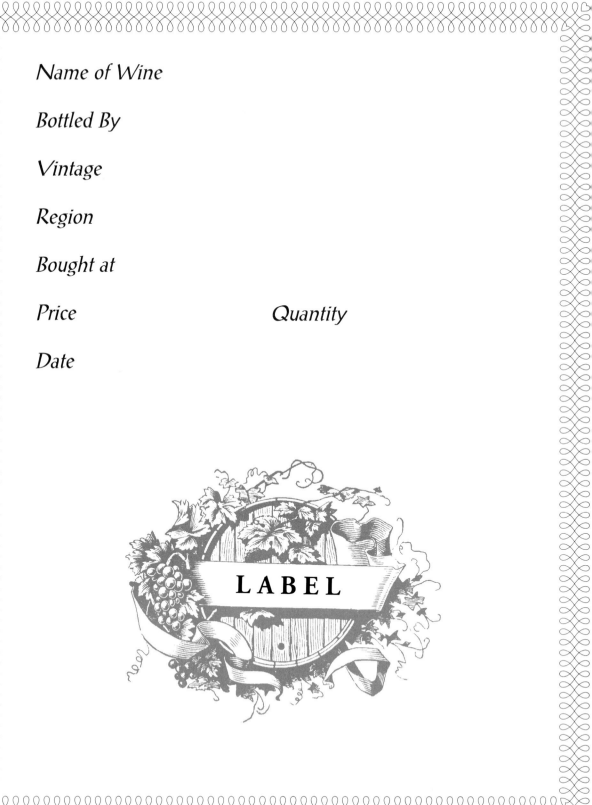

LABEL

Opened on

Place

Menu

Color

Bouquet

Taste

Remarks

Name of Wine

Bottled By

Vintage

Region

Bought at

Price   Quantity

Date

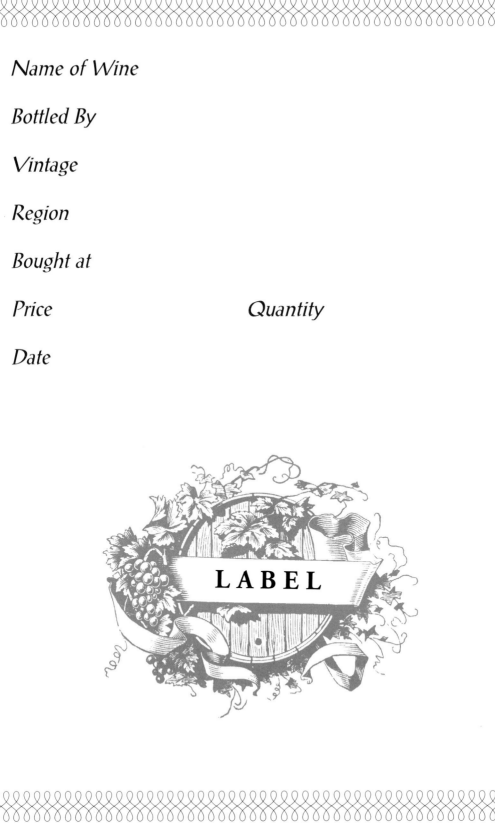

LABEL

Opened on

Place

Menu

Color

Bouquet

Taste

Remarks

FIRESIDE
Rockefeller Center
1230 Avenue of the Americas
New York, NY 10020

Designed by Jill Weber

Manufactured in the United States of America

5 7 9 10 8 6

ISBN 0-684-83222-4